Tattered
Treasures
for Your Garden

Tattered Treasures

for Your Garden

Lauren Powell

Sterling Publishing Co., Inc.
New York

PROLIFIC IMPRESSIONS PRODUCTION STAFF:

Editor in Chief: Mickey Baskett
Copy Editor: Phyllis Mueller
Graphics: Dianne Miller, Karen Turpin
Photography: Jerry Mucklow, Pat Molnar, David Bjurstrom
Administration: Jim Baskett

Every effort has been made to insure that the information presented is accurate. Since we have no control over physical conditions, individual skills, or chosen tools and products, the publisher disclaims any liability for injuries, losses, untoward results, or any other damages which may result from the use of the information in this book. Thoroughly read the instructions for all products used to complete the projects in this book, paying particular attention to all cautions and warnings shown for that product to ensure their proper and safe use.

Library of Congress Cataloging-in-Publication Data Available

10 9 8 7 6 5 4 3 2 1

Published by Sterling Publishing Company, Inc.
387 Park Avenue South, New York, N.Y. 10016

Produced by Prolific Impressions, Inc.
160 South Candler St., Decatur, GA 30030

© 2002 by Prolific Impressions, Inc.

Distributed in Canada by Sterling Publishing
c/o Canadian Manda Group, One Atlantic Avenue, Suite 105
Toronto, Ontario, Canada M6K 3E7
Distributed in Australia by Capricorn Link (Australia) Pty. Ltd.
P.O. Box 704, Winsor, NSW 2756 Australia

Printed in China
All rights reserved
Sterling ISBN 0-8069-6867-2

A Special Thank You: to the following manufacturers and shops who were so generous in providing supplies, projects, and expertise.

Nature's Pressed Flowers
P.O. Box 212
Orem, UT 84059
800-850-2499
www.naturespressed.com
For flowers on decoupaged plates

Plaid Enterprises, Inc.
P.O. Box 7600
Norcross, GA 30092
800-842-4197
www.plaidonline.com
For FolkArt Acrylic Paints and Crackle Medium, Mod Podge, Decorator Glaze, Make-It Mosaics and Faster Plaster products

Old Edna Says, "Well...La de Da!"
Crossroads of Hwy. 227 and Price Canyon Rd.
San Luis Obispo, CA 93401
805-544-8062
www.ladedaonline.com
for allowing us to photograph their shop

Ron's Nursery
1207 S. 13th Street
Grover Beach, CA 93433
805-489-4747
www.ronsnursery.com
For plants and flowers for Edna's Cottage – styling by Pam Langfeldt

Cynthia's Place
12003 High Star
Houston, TX 77072
Email: cynhorwitz@aol.com
For birdhouses

About Lauren Powell

Lauren Powell's background in art and design led to her interest in home decorating and her love of collecting. Working for the leading arts and crafts products manufacturer in the world, Plaid Enterprises, Inc., for over 15 years has created many opportunities for Lauren to gain product knowledge from leading designers. She has, for example, discovered many ways to update and add artistic touches to flea market finds through painted finishes, decoupage, mosaics, and more.

Lauren's home has been featured in *Woman's Day* and *Romantic Homes* magazines as well as on *The Kitty Bartholomew Show* on HGTV. She was also a guest on *The Christopher Lowell Show.*

Lauren lives in Austin, Texas with her husband and two children. She enjoys Bible studies and spending time with her family and her horse, Patrick. She is grateful for the opportunities in her life to share her talent and help others find theirs.

Photo credit: Miller Photography, St. Simons Island, GA

DEDICATION

A special thank you to my husband and two children for being supportive of all of my endeavors. Without their support, this book would not have become a reality.

ACKNOWLEDGEMENTS

The best part of writing books is not sitting at my computer typing away, but searching for wonderful locations and making new friends. I have realized that people are the happiest when they are able to share their passions with others. That passion was communicated quite clearly when I met the homeowners and gardeners featured in this book.

I knew from the moment that I drove past Nancy and Guy Carter's charming garden that it would be a treat to visit. The St. Simons Island, Georgia garden cleverly incorporates interesting found objects in unique and unusual ways — it is a tropical haven that anyone would enjoy. Nancy and Guy credit their friend Candace Brewer, ASLA for encouraging them to be free in expressing their personal style.

Mark and Ann Rogers, also of St. Simons Island, Georgia have taken their love of New England style and formal gardens and created a beautiful blend of their own. Their lovely cottage garden includes rustic touches such as old wheelbarrows and tools and

fanciful arbors. My favorite area is a perfectly painted cottage shed for planting, complete with flowering window boxes.

My friend Eileen Paulin led me to some of her favorite locations in California. Eileen's expert eye and creative talents are displayed in every issue of *Romantic Homes* magazine, where she is Editor. One special recommendation was an inspiring shop named *Old Edna Says, "Well...La de Da!"* owned by Judy Watkins and Pattea Torrence in San Luis Obispo, California. Charming does not even begin to describe this shop, which is full of wonderful displays of new and vintage merchandise, nor does it describe Old Edna's amazingly talented owners. Judy and Pattea escorted us to several of their customers' exceptional homes that we admired and photographed.

Finally, Cynthia Horwitz inspired me with her wonderful handmade birdhouses, which are featured on pages 45-47. She was kind enough to share her treasures and teach us how to make our own.

Contents

Preface

If you are lucky, every once in a while, you may experience magic – I mean the kind of magic that involves **all your senses**. This was the kind of magic I experienced while on photo location at the shop, *Old Edna Says, "Well...La de Da!"* My eyes **saw** beauty and creativity at every turn in the shop; rescued furniture with elegant woodworking, a gorgeous enameled clock, a piece of cut crystal, flowers everywhere filling French urns and Victorian vases. I **touched** the wonderful texture of old leather, wood worn smooth from use, soft antique fabrics. I **heard** creaking screen doors, the whine of the old wood floors when you walked on them, the cooing of doves kept in a beautiful old cage behind the shop, customer oohs and ahhs over a discovery. I **smelled** the heady fragrance of age and dried flowers (much like the smell of my mother's attic). At lunch I **tasted** the bounty of the California produce in a veggie foccacia sandwich. The shop is in beautiful Edna Valley, surrounded by mountains and farms, and it is a place that should be experienced.

Above: This is the front of Old Edna Says, "Well...La de Da!" – whimsical and enhancing and filled with treasures to enjoy.

Left: The front entrance of the shop welcomes and charms customers with a display of garden ornaments as well as indoor décor.

8

Many of the photos in this book were taken at the shop and at the homes of the two shop owners, Judy and Pattea. These talented ladies have lovingly collected a usable and gorgeous selection of "pre-used" furniture and decorative items. They have combined these collectable treasures with new fabrics and a modern sensibility to create a very livable environment.

Judy and Pattea also led me to homes of several of their customers. These wonderful folks were so kind to allow us to photograph the sanctuaries they have created for their families using their collections and finds. Lovers of antiques are usually always proud to share beauty with others. I loved hearing about how and where each item was acquired, and seeing how ordinary pieces were used extraordinarily in their decorating.

It brings a sense of history and personal touch to a home that truly speaks of the spirit of the owners.

On St. Simons Island I got a taste of true Southern hospitality and charm as we photographed several gardens there. I saw how a love of the outdoors combined with decorating talent can be used to make beautiful living spaces in a garden – spaces that can be enjoyed throughout most of the year. I marveled at the sensitivity these home owners had in creating charming nooks for bird watching, clever ways to hide and disguise, places to sit and relax or have a sunset glass of wine, enchanting ways to enhance nature's garden.

I hope seeing these tableaus will inspire you to use and enjoy vintage collections in your garden.

Mickey Baskett, editor

Above: Garden tools and birdhouses arranged on a hanging shelf outside a garage window make a pretty scene. Garden tools can not only be functional but can also be elements of design.

Ordinary Items Used in Extraordinary Ways

A garden is an extension of all the human senses – nothing compares to the fragrance of flowers, a prickly stem to the touch, the soft whisper of rustling leaves or chirping creatures to the ear, or visual beauty that stimulates the eye.

In this book, we will explore how to beautify your garden in simple, dramatic ways by adding "tattered treasures" – unusual elements such as architectural pieces, rusted relics, weathered containers, charming birdhouses, mirrors, and patterned china. I hope these pages will inspire you to look beyond traditional garden furnishings and fixtures and broaden your perspective by experimenting with inexpensive flea market finds and easy-to-make projects that will create one-of-a-kind, personal gardens.

Creating a garden provides an artistic opportunity, a blank canvas waiting to be adorned with a palette of color, from the bright and cheerful hues of impatiens and sunflowers to the soft and romantic shades of roses. The arrangement and grouping of flowers, furnishings, and accessories help create the feeling you want to achieve in your space.

Discover romance and charm in the rusty, old, and slightly worn and see how using tattered treasures can help you develop great looks that express whimsy and playfulness and add elements of surprise to any style, size, or type of garden.

Finding Your Treasures

Flea markets, yard sales, and bargain centers are perfect for locating common and unusual items. Look at items not for what they are but for what they can become. Inexpensive china platters and bowls can become birdbaths. Cracked, chipped pieces of china can be used to create colorful mosaic containers. An old window can work as a divider or decorate an arbor. Try adding columns from old houses for a formal tone. Use a mirror to reflect surrounding beauty.

Be on the lookout for the less-than-perfect – imperfections make ordinary things unique, and they are usually less expensive than brand new. Seek out pieces with little flaws, such as a chair with peeling paint or a window with broken panes. Keep in mind that the pieces you collect and use outdoors will be subject to the elements. Natural wear, fading, and weathering are desirable.

Antique and flea markets can be overwhelming due to the size and sheer variety of their offerings, but they are convenient for one-stop shopping and usually offer something for everyone. From the rustic and rugged to the refined and polished, antiques and collectibles can range in price from a few dollars to thousands. I love shopping the bargain tables and rummaging through the old windows, doors, and architectural finds for elements for my garden.

Successful flea market and yard sale shopping takes practice. To make the most of your search, try these tips:

• Search the classified ads in Thursday's newspaper for week-end yard, garage, and estate sales. (Some sales begin on Friday – you don't want to miss those!) Begin with the ad that sounds most like what you are looking for, ones with the words "antiques," "household items," "bric-a-brac," or even "junk." These are the sales to attend, rather than those that advertise baby items and toys (although I've been lucky at some of those, too).

Rough and Ready is one of my favorite spots in Austin, Texas.

- Consider mapping a route and making a plan of attack based on time and location. Start with the earliest sale and go from there to surrounding areas.

- Plan to arrive at a sale at least 30 minutes before the stated opening time to be at the front of the line. First come, first served is usually the case. At many estate sales, a line forms at the door and people are allowed in one small group at a time.

- Be advised that if the ad says "no early birds" the door won't open until the advertised time. You may not want to waste time waiting while you could be browsing somewhere else unless

Old doors, windows, columns, and posts make great garden embellishments.

you're sure there's something you really want.

- Whether you visit flea markets or garage sales, dress for comfort and wear shoes that protect your feet.

- If you love it, don't hesitate. I have discovered that it is a good idea, whether at a garage sale or flea market, to give in to your impulse if you find something you really love. If you wait too long, chances are your find will be found by someone else.

- Bring a tape measure, a notebook, a flashlight for early morning hunting, and plenty of cash!

Creating
Garden Rooms
for Living

Your patio, porch, deck, and the special places you create in your garden are extensions of your home. Outdoor spaces can be as formal and stylish or relaxed and cozy as indoor rooms. The colors of nature – found in flowers, trees, and shrubs – provide the background. With the addition of textures from furniture, fabrics, and accents, garden rooms can take on distinctive personalities.

Some spots naturally lend themselves to embellishment – areas with thick foliage or overhanging trees and branches are good places to start. Small, tucked away spaces – like those in the curve of a flower or shrub border – also work well.

Study your outdoor area to locate a spot in the yard or on the patio, porch, or deck that visually forms an enclosed and inviting niche. If you don't have such an area, create one by massing potted plants of different shapes, sizes, and textures or think about adding some structure with a fence or a lattice wall. Add height and depth with tall trees and low-lying greenery. Once you've chosen the spot, try grouping some chairs for a cozy seating arrangement. Add a table – large or small – to make a lovely outdoor dining area. Plants in pots and containers nestled among the furniture help separate areas and provide added color and additional texture.

At right: An arbor becomes a shady shelter. Comfy pillows made from old fabrics and a colorful old quilt add to the cozy feeling of this resting place. A closet near the back door holds the pillows and quilt each night. A window is hung in this nook to give the illusion of a room.

An Outdoor French Café

Garden rooms can be decorated to emulate specific styles. The iron furniture and blue-and-white checked tablecloth of this outdoor dining area, *right,* are reminiscent of an outdoor French café. The space is surrounded with plants to give it borders and make it feel more intimate. An old iron standing candelabra has been painted blue and is used during twilight dining.

A Beach Cottage Porch

This authentic tabby house has a delightful porch, *below,* filled with shade-loving green plants and white-painted wicker furniture. A painted metal container on the door holds cut flowers. The blue and white color scheme of the chair cushions is echoed by the mosaic on a cement urn, which is made of broken pieces of blue and white china.

A Deck That Overlooks a Garden

Pillows, throws, and other soft furnishings can make a deck feel like a room, and using watering cans and garden tools as accessories extends the garden theme. Here, painted metal garden chairs are pulled up around an old drop-leaf dining table whose legs have been shortened to coffee-table height. A woven fiber rug pulls the grouping together.

Rather than building a new wooden railing for the deck, this homeowner chose to incorporate a balustrade rescued from the front porch of an old house. The peeling white paint gives the balustrade a less formal appearance, underscoring the casual setting. With this railing addition, the new deck takes on the appearance of having been a part of this old house.

If the area is sheltered from rain, you can enjoy using pillows, cushions, throws, or rugs anytime. Otherwise, plan on storing them nearby for easy access on sunny days.

Natural floor treatments are the foundations of garden rooms. Brick and flagstone are easy to lay and beautiful to look at. Wooden decks and platforms provide a smooth, level surface for furnishings. Other simple, attractive options include grass, gravel, pebbles, and stone.

An interesting mix of textures – the weathered brick floor, lattice walls, and iron, wicker, wood, and glass furniture – makes this garden room, *left,* inviting. Touches of color come from oversized pillows in floral-patterned fabrics and blooming potted plants.

A Welcoming Display for Guests

Create a welcoming first impression on your front porch and greet guests with a seasonal display, *below*. In the autumn, let pumpkins and a colorful arrangement of leaves, pods, grasses, and fragrant eucalyptus spill out of an old wheelbarrow. Upholstered furniture is unexpected outdoors, further extending the idea that the visitor has entered a room.

A Porch Furnished Like an Entry Hall

A sheltered front porch, *right*, can be furnished like an entry hall with a cabinet and a bench for seating. Here, a painted wooden cupboard with a weathered finish holds an arrangement of potted plants, cut flowers, a rustic birdhouse, and a miniature metal lawn chair. A wood-and-metal park bench with peeling paint provides a place to sit and a resting place for packages.

Entertaining Outdoors

When you have created a comfortable space in your garden, invite friends and family to enjoy it with you. For special occasions, bring indoor items outside. Toss colorful pillows and cushions into chairs and drape linens over tables to soften their lines. White damask feels more dressy and formal; quilts impart a relaxed, country feel.

Whether your food plans include a sit-down dinner or an appetizer buffet, concentrate on creating a beautiful presentation. Mis-matched china or hand-made decoupaged dishes will delight your guests. Roll vintage cloth or beautiful paper napkins and tie them with raffia and a fresh sprig of greenery. Baskets and buckets make eye-catching containers. Don't forget fresh flowers for the centerpiece.

Here, a red-and-white color scheme unifies a collection of pillows, *right*, in vintage (and vintage-inspired) fabrics – toile, ticking, gingham. A white tablecloth with cotton crochet trim is draped casually over the table. Assorted cloth napkins, rolled and tied with jute twine, are gathered in a painted metal colander. A bouquet of lilies fills a tall French bucket.

A bench constructed from recycled wood, *below*, is reminiscent of an old church pew. When paired with a weathered farm table, it's the foundation for a festive garden party.

Make-It-Yourself

WILDFLOWER DECOUPAGED PLATES

Dry and pressed garden flowers — from your own garden or purchased from a craft store — are used to create lovely decoupaged plates that add an elegant touch to your outdoor entertaining.

You'll Need:

Clear glass plates

Dried and pressed flowers and
    leaves

Decoupage medium

Small paintbrush

Tweezers

Thin handmade paper

Here's How:

1. Wash and dry plates.

2. Working on the backside of plate, apply a thin coat of decoupage medium to the center area of the plate.

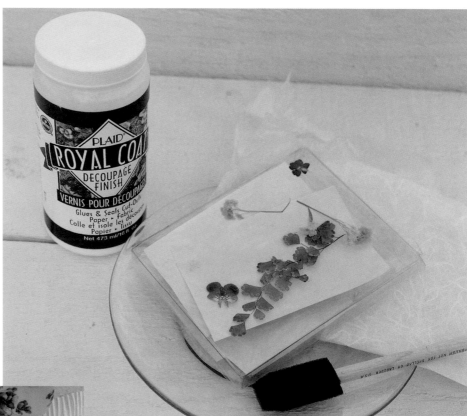

3. While the medium is still wet, pick up flowers, one at a time, with tweezers and arrange them, face down, on the center of the plate. You may need to apply more decoupage medium as you build layers of flowers and leaves.

4. Apply decoupage medium around the rim of the plate on the backside. Add flowers, again using tweezers and placing the flowers one at a time. Allow to dry in place.

5. Tear handmade paper into small strips. Brush strips with decoupage medium. Place overlapping strips of paper over the flowers on the back of plate until entire backside of the plate is covered with paper.

6. Coat with decoupage medium to seal. Allow to dry.

7. Turn over plate and trim away excess paper.

To use: **Do not** submerge in water or place in a dishwasher. Glass fronts of plates may be wiped clean. ❑

Candles for Entertaining Outdoors

Consider candles for illuminating an evening event. Limit the use of electric spotlights, which can look harsh and overly bright, and use lots of candles or tiki torches for a warm glow. Set large pillar candles in sand-filled terra cotta pots for quick and easy illumination, or line up small glass votives to mark a pretty pathway.

Old metal chandeliers can be beautiful candle holders – just remove the wiring and place candles where the bulb sockets once were. Use as a centerpiece or hang from a tree or pergola.

A metal candelabra, *below,* makes a wonderful garden-party centerpiece with the addition of moss and small plants.

Architectural Elements Used Creatively

Used inside or out, old windows, shutters, doors, columns, statues, parts of fences, and gates provide dramatic effects and add instant style. Salvaged items, available at most flea markets, can be used as "walls" for garden rooms. An old door lends character when wedged between trees or propped up against a solid wall. Hang window frames and sashes from trees or arbors to define an area and provide a conversation starter.

Right: Four less-than-perfect turned balusters make chunky, interesting legs for this one-of-a-kind table. The balusters are attached with screws to an iron gate, which is topped with a cut-to-fit tempered glass top with rounded corners.

Columns can do more than provide structural support. Reminiscent of grand entries and antebellum estates, columns add a touch of class and romance when nestled randomly among greenery. To shorten a column, remove the shaft from the base, cut to desired height, and reposition securely.

Old columns, *far left,* add classical elegance when tucked among greenery and flowers in the garden. Potted ferns and flowers, *left,* can provide a boundary when elevated and staggered at varying heights along terraces or on freestanding pedestals. Here, a simple square column is the perfect perch for a potted plant.

Windows are versatile, varied, and can be free for the taking – you can often find them curbside in neighborhoods where people are renovating and remodeling.

When hung in just the right spot, a window can be a work of art. In this garden room, *above,* a window frame is hung like a painting on a wall.

It appears that you are inside looking out, rather than actually being outside.

The sturdy rose trellis, *left,* was designed to incorporate an old window frame, making the new piece more interesting and giving the look of a window on a wall.

Birdhouse Retreats

Once just shelters for our feathered friends, birdhouses are "must-have" decorative accents for the garden. Whether simple or fanciful, rustic or ornate, they are symbols of home and safe haven and opportunities for small-scale artistic expression.

No longer just for the birds, these creative houses can be found in as many styles as there are species. Birdhouse styles vary from classic to country, oriental to contemporary. They may be made of iron, wood (plank and twig), metal, gourd, or bamboo.

Right: Birdhouses mounted on fence posts or columns can create a whimsical focal point. A grouping – a birdhouse village, if you please – is more dramatic and visually interesting than just one.

An assortment of brass drawer pulls and a jeweled filigree ornament embellish the walls of this square birdhouse, *above*. Outdoors, the copper roof will soon acquire a characteristic green patina. (The same effect can be created on a wooden roof with a paint kit from a crafts store.) A brass finial shines on top.

This weathered, well-used birdhouse sits on a metal bracket that's mounted on a tree, *right*. (A piece of white-covered wire adds additional stability.) The metal-topped cupola supports a metal spring topped with a painted star. The bracket also supports an old tin pot used as a hanging planter.

Doorknobs, odd pieces of hardware, old tin, gate finials, and old pieces of trim can be used to embellish simple birdhouse shapes, *below*. Embellishments like scraps of picture molding, a carved cherub, cast resin architectural trims, and metal pieces are harmonized with white paint and recall classic architecture. Metal – even painted metal – will rust over time outdoors.

Paint finishes such as crackling and antiquing can make a new birdhouse look old.

The shapes and colors of painted birdhouses are the repeated motif in this garden display, *right*. Rusty tin boxes, flower pots and planters, and an old wooden bowling pin – just one – are part of the interesting mix of textures and shapes.

Simple or elaborate, a birdhouse in the garden is attractive to humans as well as wildlife. The many colors and styles available offer something for every design preference. Regardless of the style, they complement any garden environment.

Using Birdhouses Indoors

Brought indoors, birdhouses add architectural interest and a garden motif to any room. They are dramatic accents when placed atop a cabinet or armoire.

Make-It-Yourself

BUILD & PAINT A BIRDHOUSE

Making birdhouses can be as enjoyable as seeing them displayed in the garden. Using old painted boards, you can easily create birdhouses with the warm, rustic appeal that comes with years of age and exposure to the elements. Salvaged architectural pieces extend the vintage theme – use what you can find: old flatware, fence pickets, rusty keys. Perfection isn't necessary, or desirable. Birdhouses designed by Cynthia Horwitz.

Right: This birdhouse chapel started with a simple basic shape. A piece of wood mounted on the tin roof forms the steeple, topped with a cross made from discarded flatware. A large nail driven at the center of a doorknob rose is used as a perch. Trim pieces suggest windows and doors.

MAKING A BIRDHOUSE

These basic instructions can be adapted to any design. Sizes of boards can be altered to create different heights and widths. Get creative with embellishments. To protect your feathered friends, place tin-roofed birdhouses in shady areas – they can get very hot inside if placed in direct sun.

You'll Need:

Wooden boards (recycled siding, shelving, etc.)

Two pieces, 6" wide x 10" high (for the front and back walls)

Two pieces, 8" wide x 6" high (for the side walls)

Two 2" x 8" (for sides)

One 6" x 13" (for the bottom)

One 4-1/2" piece of 2" wide molding

Old piece of tin (roofing, ceiling tile, etc.)

Nails

Wood glue

Decorative Accents

Optional: Paint and paint brush

Tools:

Hammer

1-1/2" spade drill bit

Hand or electric drill

Saw

Right: A rectangular door plate makes a fanciful "door" on this birdhouse. Other decorations include old keys, a gate finial, and a piece of cast metal.

46

Left: A white china doorknob and a coat hook serve as perches. Old soup spoons placed on the front echo the pitch of the birdhouse roof.

Here's How:

1. Cut a point on one end of each front and back piece to form the roof angle. Start the angle 6" up from one end so the walls minus the roof gable are 6" tall.

2. Run a bead of glue down the inside edges of the back piece where sides will join. Nail one side piece to each side of the back piece.

3. Run a bead of glue down the inside of the front piece and nail to side pieces.

4. Run a bead of glue around bottom piece and nail to front back and sides.

5. Fold the tin piece and glue in place on the top of the birdhouse, letting it overhang on the sides.

6. *Optional:* To make a steeple, cut a small piece of wood or molding to match the angle of the roof. Glue to the roof. Attach a piece of scrap tin with glue for the steeple roof.

7. Use a 1-1/2" spade bit to drill an entrance hole on the front.

8. *Optional:* Paint birdhouse.

9. Hammer a 16-penny nail for a perch under the entrance hole.

10. Embellish with decorative elements such as silverware, keys, tin pieces, etc. ❏

Mirrors,
Glass & China
in the Garden

Enjoy and magnify the splendor of your garden with the
addition of reflective and patterned surfaces. Mirrors, glass,
and china all work wonderfully as accents to enhance the
surrounding beauty. Mirrors can be hung on fences, shed
walls, the side of a house, or even trees. Pay attention to
what the mirror reflects, and use the reflected image to
visually enlarge your favorite areas.

Mirrors are available in a variety of shapes and sizes – it's the
frame that makes each mirror unique and determines the
style. Rustic iron frames suggest old world charm, while
weathered wood frames denote a country look.

*At right: Treat the birds to a cool splash in this birdbath made from an old china platter.
The small porcelain bird was glued to the platter with epoxy glue from the hardware store.*

Directly outside the backdoor of this California cottage, the owner created an elegant retreat.
A raised pond with fountain was constructed and is sheltered by an elaborate wooden trellis,
complete with roof. In a few years vines will cover the trellis, making the spot even more
intimate. A wooden fireplace mantel surrounds a mirror that reflects the dramatic beauty
of a fountain.

Using Mirrors

A cast arched-top metal grille – probably from a 19th century coal fireplace – and a framed oval mirror adorn a blank wall on a tabby beach cottage, *above left*. Be sure to slant mirrors to protect birds from flying into them.

A mirror cut to shape and installed behind a gothic arched window frame reflects the garden before it and the window's ornamental metal window guard, creating the illusion of a window on a lattice wall, *above right*.

Its glass long gone, an old window sash, *right*, has a new life as a mirror. Salvaged architectural elements set above and a ledge below lend embellishment and room for displays.

Using Glass

Glass can be used in the garden for color, texture, and function. The many colors of glass – from emerald green and cobalt blue to earthy tones of brown and frost – can stand out boldly or blend in subtly. Old wine bottles planted neck down in the ground form unique borders for beds and pathways. Glass domes or cloches are ideal for creating terrariums and protecting tender plants. Glass doorknobs can be fanciful garden stakes, decorative embellishments on birdhouses, or hangers when attached to a wooden post or plaque. Any tree can have colorful blooms when small bottles are attached with wire to branches and filled with flowers.

Using China

The garden is the perfect place to use slightly chipped or faded china – you don't need to invest in fine, expensive pieces for outdoor dining and decorating. Colorful floral patterns work naturally in a garden. Collect pieces with a common theme or color palette; lonely, mismatched pieces are waiting to be purchased at bargain prices. When you've gathered a set of complementary patterns, shapes, or themes, show them off at an alfresco dinner party or reception.

Not just for dining anymore, china plates can add color and pattern to walls. Shallow china bowls and platters make luxurious, elegant birdbaths when mounted on a pedestal or placed on a tree stump.

Use garden cloches, the tops of glass cake servers, or cheese domes to shelter tender plants and coax cuttings of favorite plants to root. The glass magnifies the beauty underneath and provides protection for tender rootings.

Small willowware china and blue and white soap dishes are the perfect decorative accents for this shower enclosure at a beach cottage. The blue-tinted stain on the wood plank walls echoes the colors of the plates. Iron hinges and a white china knob, used as the door pull, extend the cottage theme. The moon-shaped cutout on the door adds a playful touch.

Mosaics in the Garden

Broken china can be recycled to make mixed media mosaics that decorate furniture, sculptures, or stepping stones. Decorative mosaics created with broken materials, such as china, tile, and glass, are named "picassiette" after Maison Picassiette, a cottage in Chartres, France where all the surfaces, including the furniture and a woodstove, were covered with shards of colorful crockery, glass, stones, and shells.

Pieces of broken blue and white china and small blue tiles add life and pattern to concrete stepping stones, *right*.

See page 58 for instructions on making stepping stones

Make-It-Yourself

MOSAICS FOR THE GARDEN

Use chipped or broken china, tiles, and marbles to create one-of-a-kind stepping stones and decorative accents. The same basic technique can be used to create mosaics on other surfaces, such as terra cotta flowerpots or wooden frames. Flat surfaces are easier to work with than rounded or curved ones. Use caution when breaking tiles and china – the pieces can be sharp. Always wear eye protection and gloves when breaking and working with broken china and tiles, and be sure to cover your mouth and nose with a dust mask when mixing grout.

You'll Need:

A smooth surface (cement stepping stone or terra cotta pot – both are available at garden centers)

China plates or tiles

Sanded grout

Silicone glue

Tools & Other Equipment

Hammer or rubber mallet

Goggles or other eye protection

Towels

Several sponges

Plastic container (for mixing grout)

Paint stick or other disposable tool (for mixing grout)

Rubber gloves

Rubber spatula

Dust mask

Soft cloth

Optional: Tile nippers, acrylic paint, mosaic sealer

Use nippers to trim pieces to size.

Glue pieces in place on surface.

Spread grout on surface, making sure it fills in crevices between china pieces.

Here's How:

1. Place china plates between two towels or newspaper. Tap with a hammer to break. Continue until you have enough pieces to cover most of surface. Tile nippers can be used to break or trim pieces to size needed.

2. First plan the placement of your china pieces and trim as necessary.

3. Glue pieces on surface by spreading glue on the back of a piece of china. Place the pieces no more than 1/4" apart. Allow to dry until secure (about 24 hours).

4. Mix grout in a disposable container according to manufacturer's instructions. Grout can be tinted any color by adding acrylic paint to mixture.

5. Wearing rubber gloves, use a spatula to apply grout over the glued china pieces, pressing the grout into the crevices between the pieces, making sure all areas are filled and level.

6. Use a damp sponge to wipe away excess grout. Let dry for at least one hour.

7. Buff with a soft cloth to remove the cloudy residue. Let dry completely (about 48 hours).

8. Seal grout for outdoor use. ❏

Wipe off excess grout with a sponge.

Garden
Accents

Use creative accents in the garden to bring unexpected color, texture, shine, and whimsy. An "accent" can be virtually anything that appeals to you, is satisfying to the eye, and can (at least for a while) stand up to the rigors of the elements.

Take a look around your home and notice your collections and favorite treasures. If you collect roosters, why not take a few outside? If blue and white china is your passion, bring some outdoors.

Arranged in groups or positioned by themselves, creative accents add charm and personality to any space. Don't worry about rules or tradition – have fun and personalize!

At right: Decorative ceramic balls look like fanciful flowers when used as garden accents. These can be used to stake flowers or simply used as ornamentation. The ceramic balls can be found at import stores. Ann Rogers created these garden ornaments by using epoxy to glue a long nail onto the ceramic balls. The nail was inserted into a hollow bamboo stalk.

Small items such as decorative molding and fretwork, knobs, door and drawer pulls, decorative hardware, finials, and hooks can be used and combined with other materials to make functional items that add artistic emphasis to the garden. Glass and china doorknobs and drawer pulls make lovely garden stakes when joined to copper piping. Antique hot and cold water faucets become hooks for hats and hoses when screwed into plywood, and randomly applied drawer pulls embellish cute houses for the birds. Items such as concrete statues and terra cotta pots add beautiful ornamentation to the garden, especially when they are old or purposely aged with paint.

Use heavy duty glue or epoxy to affix iron, plastic, or ceramic elements to fence post finials, *right*. A garden stake made from a copper pipe and a glass drawer pull supports a blooming gladiola, *left & below*. See page 64 for instructions on how to make it.

Make-It-Yourself

ORNAMENTAL GARDEN STAKES

When challenged to find a new use for old drawer pulls, Nancy Carter came up with a delightfully whimsical approach to garden stakes. Make these wonderful accents in three easy steps.

You'll Need:

1 drawer pull with screw

Copper pipe, cut to the height you want your stake to be

1 lag shield, to fit the diameter of the pipe (from the hardware store)

Here's How:

1. Insert lag shield about half way into one end of the copper pipe while holding the other end.

2. Place the end of the drawer pull screw into the end of the lag shield you are holding. Turn the screw. The lag shield will begin to open as you turn the screw, expanding against the inside of the pipe.

3. Continue to turn the screw, pushing the lag shield into pipe until secure. ❏

A Collection of Flower Frogs

Usually hidden in the bottoms of containers to assist with floral arrangements, these antique flower frogs, *below*, have come out of hiding to be part of the centerpiece, holding a collection of freshly cut blooms. For best results, cut the flowers and hold in water. Arrange them just before company arrives, as some flowers wilt quickly out of water. They last longer if placed in a shady spot.

A Pressed Flower Tray

An old picture frame that displays a favorite note embellished with dried and pressed flowers makes a wonderful garden accent, *right*. Pressed flowers and handwritten notes are decoupaged to frame backing that has been painted. Attach handles to the sides of the frame to create a tray for serving and entertaining.

$\boxed{\text{Make-It-Yourself}}$

A WEATHERED SHELF WITH FAUCET HANDLE HOOKS

Liz Carter used salvaged hot and cold water faucet handles as hooks for hanging on this one-of-a-kind shelf.

You'll Need:
Old scrap lumber (the more
   weathered, the better)
1 piece, 12" wide x 24" long
   (for back panel)
1 piece, 5" wide x 28" long
   (for shelf)
2 pieces, each 4" wide x 6"
   long (for side brackets)
3 old water faucet handles
3 taps sized to fit faucets,
   1-1/2" long
3 nuts to fit taps
Finishing nails
Tape measure
Drill & drill bit
Hanger

Here's How:
Make the Shelf:
1. Nail one side bracket to end of the back panel.

2. Center the shelf on the top edge of the back panel. Nail to back and side brackets. (The shelf will extend past the side brackets.)

Attach the Faucets:
1. Measure and mark placement for three holes that are equally spaced along the back panel.

2. Drill holes slightly larger than the taps at marks on the board.

3. Attach one faucet handle to one end of a tap and screw to secure.

4. Slide tap through one of the holes. Secure with a nut on the back. Repeat to attach other two faucet handles.

5. Attach hanger on back. ❑

Concrete
Decorations

Seen in gardens all over the world, concrete decorations add character to garden spaces. Used to mark an entryway or snuggled deep into a flowerbed, a concrete statue adds a traditional touch – popular subjects include cherubs and angels, bunnies, dogs, urns, and baskets. Don't pass up a broken one; a fragment of a statue can be as effective as the whole thing.

Concrete is one thing that gets better with age. Moss-covered and weathered surfaces are appealing and desired. (You can use a preparation from a garden center or crafts store to achieve this effect if you are too impatient to wait on nature.)

At right: A concrete birdbath displays a collection of treasures from the sea.

$\boxed{\text{Make-It-Yourself}}$

AGING CONCRETE

New concrete pieces can be made to look old with muriatic acid etching and thinned acrylic paint. Work outdoors and shield your work area with plenty of old newspapers or a large dropcloth to protect from overspray. The technique also can be used on painted concrete pieces to give them an aged appearance.

When you're finished aging your piece, you can protect it from further aging with a sealer or let nature take its course.

You'll Need:

Concrete piece

Muriatic acid (sold at hardware and building supply stores)

Acrylic craft paint - black or dark brown

Optional: Non-yellowing clear matte sealer spray or polyurethane

Tools & Other Supplies:

Spray bottle

Newspapers or drop cloth for work area

Water

Large paint brush

Rubber gloves

Glasses or eye goggles

Rags

Here's How:

1. Place concrete piece on newspapers or dropcloth.

2. Pour muriatic acid into a spray bottle and spray concrete piece. The muriatic acid will eat away the concrete and form small pits and an uneven appearance. Allow to dry. Repeat the process until desired look is achieved.

3. Mix one part black or umber paint with one part water and brush over concrete piece. Wipe away excess with rags. Allow the dark color to seep into the cracks, crevices, and pits on concrete. Several applications may be needed, as the porous surface will absorb the thinned paint. Let dry.

4. *Option:* Spray with sealer or polyurethane. Let dry. ❏

At right: Concrete containers are not just for the garden. Aged concrete planters are a beautiful accessory in a sunroom or on a covered porch.

Make-It-Yourself

CONCRETE WITH A FAUX WOOD FINISH

Concrete can imitate wood when primed, painted, and rubbed with a brown umber glaze.

You'll Need:
Concrete piece
Primer (choose a white-
    pigmented primer
    compatible with oil-base
    paint)
Oil-base paints - antique
    white, brown umber
Mineral spirits
Large paint brush
Rags

Here's How:
1. Brush primer over entire concrete piece. Allow to dry.

2. Paint entire piece with antique white oil-base paint. Allow to dry.

3. Thin brown umber paint with mineral spirits to make a transparent wash. Using a large paintbrush, apply the brown wash to the primed and painted surface, pushing the dark color into cracks and crevices with the brush. Wipe away excess with dry rags.

4. Repeat until the effect pleases you. ❑

Faded, chipped, and pitted – but loaded with character and charm – this spiraling, scroll-like volute from an old concrete column adds classical appeal to a garden setting.

A sand cast ornament adds old-world charm when hung on a fence post in the garden. See page 16 for instructions to make it yourself.

Make-It-Yourself

SAND CAST CONCRETE ORNAMENT

*Sand casting is an age-old art form that uses a form pressed into damp sand to make
a mold. Sand cast pieces are easy to make and will remind you of sunny days and sandy shores.
My friend Pam Kerr taught me this technique. You can use plaster of paris to cast pieces you
plan to use on a sheltered porch or indoors (they need to be protected from direct rain and
moisture). Be sure to wear a face mask when mixing dusty ingredients such as concrete,
plaster of paris, or grout.*

You'll Need:

Concrete mix or plaster of paris

25 lbs. (one bag) fine white sand

Architectural piece (flat items with carved or molded details work well) to use to make the mold

Large container (for holding sand – deep enough to accommodate the architectural piece)

Bucket for mixing plaster

Plastic cups

Stirring utensils

Face mask

Florist wire cut into 2" pieces

Here's How:

1. Put sand in the container. Add enough water to make the sand damp. It should stick together and hold its shape when you squeeze a handful, but should not be soggy.

2. Press the architectural piece into the sand to create an impression. (This makes the mold for your casting.) Remove carefully so as not to disrupt the impression. You can make as many impressions as will fit in your container without crowding.

3. Mix concrete according to package instructions. Do not over-stir or the mix will harden too quickly and you will not be able to pour. (If you're using plaster of paris, the mixture should resemble cream soup.)

4. Use a cup to dip the mix from the bucket and pour it into the sand cast molds.

5. Bend pieces of wire into U-shapes to make hanger loops. Place the loops in the molded piece. Let set. Plaster will undergo a chemical process – it will get warm and then turn cool. It is ready to remove from the sand when it is cold and hard.

6. Carefully scoop the molded piece out of the sand. Lightly brush off excess sand and let dry thoroughly. ❏

Press into sand. *Add embellishments.* *Pour concrete.*

Fences
Gates
& Arbors

Fences, gates, and arbors define garden spaces. The choices are many – stained planks, pickets and balusters (with peeling paint or not), delicate ironwork, natural twigs – select a style to complement your home and your garden.

A white picket fence has a cottage look, while a stained or natural wood one looks country. The detailed workmanship of wrought iron is strong and elegant – it can be simple and rustic or elaborate and formal.

Gates can be made of the same material as the fence, but using a different material may lend just the right effect. An old iron gate, hung on a wall or fence, makes a terrific trellis.

An arbor adds height and importance to an entry. Covered in clinging vines and crowned with sweet-scented flowers, a beautiful arbor can be an enchanting focal point.

At right: A new deck cleverly incorporates a salvaged balustrade. The homeowners chose to leave the old, peeling paint alone, rather than scraping and re-painting. In the autumn, the railing is decorated with a procession of colorful mini pumpkins.

A Fence Defines a Garden Patch

A scarecrow, arms outstretched, guards the gate to a fenced garden patch. The curved tops of the swinging gate frame the scarecrow. The black iron strap hinges are simple and complement the plank pickets.

In another garden, a less menacing scarecrow stands guard within a picketed enclosure. The pickets on the fence are more widely spaced than those on the gate. Vines have been allowed to grow up and over an arbor, creating a charming bower.

Other rustic touches include teepee-style twig trellises, an old wooden wheelbarrow, a concrete statue, and a birdbath set at ground level. The hanging basket on the gate further embellishes the entry. White flowers coordinate with the scarecrow's white clothes.

This weathered whitewashed gate and arbor, *left*, are overflowing with creeping vines that soften the formal construction. A grouping of birdhouses, a blue glass fishing buoy, and a profusion of flowers add to the cottage look.

The homeowners brought this graceful iron gate, *below*, back from a trip to England. The blue paint is unexpected and lively, since most iron fences and gates are black. A cast brass coat-of-arms medallion was added to the gate, and a small brass bird sits on the fence post to welcome visitors, *right*.

Make-It-Yourself

TWIG ARBOR

This simply constructed curved twig arbor is covered with Sweet Autumn clematis. The form is built with 4 x 4 posts and flexible PVC pipe and is covered with an assortment of branches, small trees, and limbs. Galvanized baling wire holds everything together.

You'll Need:
Two 4 ft. x 4 ft.
   pressure-treated wooden
   posts, 12 ft. tall
Galvanized baling wire
Two flexible PVC pipes,
   1" diameter, 12 ft. long
Lots of fresh branches,
   saplings, or small limbs of
   various sizes
Concrete for setting posts
Clematis or other vines

Tools & Equipment
Posthole digger

1. Determine the placement of the arbor and where the posts should be. (Plan to place them 5 to 6 ft. apart.)

2. With a posthole digger, dig a hole for each post. The holes should be 2 ft. deep.

3. Place posts in holes and pack dirt back around posts to secure *or* set in concrete, following manufacturer's instructions.

4. Once posts are secure, create the arch of the arbor with the two lengths of PVC pipe. Secure pipes, one at a time, with baling wire to one post, placing the pipe about 2 ft. from the top of the post. Bend to create the arch desired.

5. Working one pipe at a time, use baling wire to secure the pipes to the other post, again placing the pipe about 2 ft. down from top with galvanized baling wire.

6. Once the form is complete, secure branches, saplings, and limbs to the form with baling wire to camouflage the PVC pipes and posts.

7. Plant vines in the ground at the base of the arbor and tie or wrap around limbs. ❏

Garden Seating

Restful and relaxing seating areas in the garden will prove to be favorite retreats for you and your guests. A small settee or bench surrounded by beautiful flowers and trees is the perfect place for quiet time or study. An intimate grouping of two chairs offers a place for friends to sit and chat. Bring out a few pillows for added comfort.

*At right: In a scene reminiscent of Provence, a lacy-looking antique iron bench adds timeless grace to an island cottage garden near a planting of chaste tree (**Vitex agnus-castus**). Stained shutters, blooming flowers, mosaic stepping stones, and a mosaic-trimmed birdbath add color to the scene.*

Capture the garden style indoors – a wooden garden bench and a watering can find a home indoors in a warm and sunny spot, *above*. Fresh white paint – on the bench, the table, the watering can, and the basket that holds a quilt – unifies the look.

A collection of salvaged treasures form a garden vignette, *right*. The legs of the bench came from an old kitchen stove; its seat and backrest are made of painted wood. On the backrest, the piece of the stove that held a clock now displays the lid from a china dish. For stability, the bench's legs rest on stepping stones. A metal smoking stand that once held an ashtray now holds a potted plant. The candelabra is used in the evenings for light.

Make-It-Yourself

WEATHERING WOOD

You can instantly antique or add color to your garden furniture with simple paint techniques. A wooden surface takes on a new hue with a color wash. Sanding and glazing create an aged look.

COLOR WASHING

A color wash is simply an application of thinned paint brushed over a surface. Choose any color you like, and feel free to experiment with the ratio of paint to water in your wash mix.

You'll Need:
Unfinished wooden furniture
Sandpaper
Latex paint
Paint brush, 3-4" wide
Plastic container
Rags
Water
Optional: Sealer

Here's How:
1. Sand the unfinished wood surface to smooth. Wipe away dust.

2. Thin latex paint with water in a plastic container – use about half paint and half water. Try your mix on a piece of scrap wood. If the mix is too thin (transparent), add more paint. If the mix is too thick (opaque), add more water.

3. Dip the brush in the paint mix and brush quickly over the wood surface. Have a damp rag available for drips or to wipe away excess. Work quickly, as the wood will absorb the paint like it would a stain. Let dry.

4. Adjust the color – if it's too dark or opaque, sand the surface to remove some of the paint. If the color seems too transparent, add a bit more paint to the wash mixture and brush on a second coat. Let dry.

5. *Option:* Seal the surface. ❑

At left: Naturally aged and weathered pieces gently blend with the elements of nature, but if you can't find a gently worn piece that has just the look you want, it's easy to create a timeworn look on new wood with paint, a few tools, and sandpaper. Here, a wash of paint adds weathering and a fun hue to an Adirondack chair.

AGING & ANTIQUING

To create instant age on wood, use layers of acrylic paint and wax such as clear or white candle or canning wax (paraffin), which is sold at grocery and hardware stores. (Do not use colored candle wax – the candle dye could bleed through the paint.) When sanded, all the paint colors will show.

You'll Need:

Acrylic paint, one or more
   colors of your choice

Wax (see above)

Paint brushes

Paint scraper

Sandpaper, 220 grit

Antiquing glaze

Here's How:

1. *Option:* Apply one to three coats of a base color. Let dry.

2. Apply wax to surface with the grain of the wood, concentrating wax in areas where paint would most likely be worn away by handling, such as edges.

3. Apply one to three additional coats of paint – the same color or different colors. Let dry between coats. **Do not sand** between coats. For a layered effect, use two or more paint colors. Allow paint to dry between colors and rub wax over the painted surface before adding the next color.

4. Scrape surface with paint scraper, working in the direction of the wood grain, to reveal the raw wood or base paint or both. In areas where wax was applied, paint will scrape off easily. Brush away excess paint particles.

5. Sand surface to smooth areas where paint has been removed.

6. Apply an antiquing glaze to mellow the effect and blend and tone down paint colors. Let dry. ❏

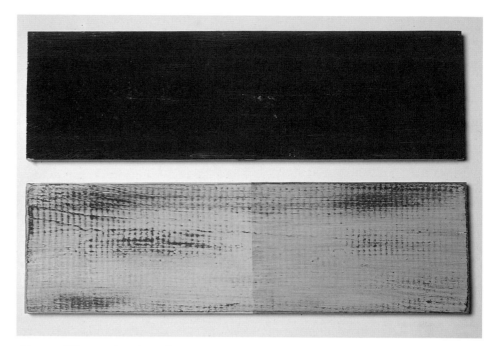

Photo 1: *This weathered wood starts out with a basecoat of deep barn red shown on the board at top. The top coat is a green/beige color. Shown at left, the top coat has been sanded. At right shows the addition of an antiquing glaze.*

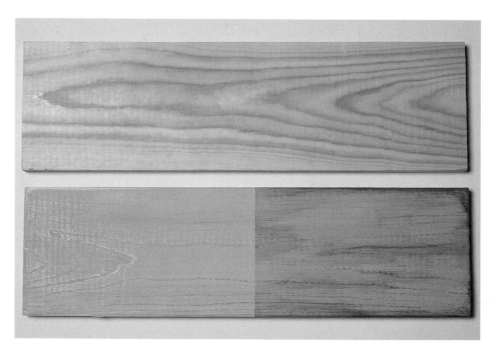

Photo 2: *This weathered wood starts with raw wood as shown with the board on top. A green/beige top coat has been added. The left side shows just sanding while the right side shows an addition of an antiquing glaze.*

Left: Naturally weathered wood on an outside garden bench.

Below: Aged finishes work nicely on accessory items as well. This new wooden tray was painted to look like an antique. A centerpiece is created by filling the tray with moss and old garden tools. A broken terra cotta pot holds a special message.

Pots,
Planters &
Watering Cans

Just about anything can become a container for
blooming plants. An old wheelbarrow, tin watering cans
and troughs – even old shoes and suitcases – make unusual
and unique planters.

Some items are easily converted for use as vases and
containers; others will need a liner or a smaller glass
container placed inside for protection. Partially fill large or
deep containers with rocks or pieces of broken terra cotta
pots to save on potting soil and provide drainage.
Containers sharing a common color or theme work well
together. For quick and easy centerpieces, group similar
items, such as baskets, pitchers, small bottles, and watering
cans, in arrangements. For variety, display arrangements of
containers made of the same material – like old gas cans and
buckets with traditional favorites like watering cans.

At right: A weathered watering can filled with flowers is a welcoming touch on a plank door.
Fresh flowers and greenery can be varied to reflect the seasons.

Above, a creative planter: An oval watering trough overflows with white impatiens. A little round white birdhouse sits neatly tucked into the blooms. The entire scene is serene and subdued – the gray of the tin echoes the weathered wooden wall. The plants were chosen for their varied textures and white-variegated foliage.

At right: A variety of containers sit ready for use in a garden shed. Terra cotta pots, tin buckets, wooden barrels, and baskets of willow, oak, and wire share space with seeds and gardening gear. Use pots, baskets, buckets, and watering cans not only to hold plants and flowers, but also as containers for other items, such as gardening tools or magazines.

Old watering cans are easy to find and fun to collect, and they're available in all sizes and shapes. They offer the romance of simpler times and fascinate us with their graceful shapes. They're versatile, too — they can be functional or decorative. When painted, they add touches of color to any room or garden style.

Antique watering cans — one with its original paint — perch in front of an iron grille, *below*. Fire-engine red paint plays up the elegant shape

of the longnecked can on the left and contrasts with the original green and yellow colors of the can next to it.

For greater visual impact, group like items together. An antique wagon, *right* is the focal point of a garden-themed display that includes four watering cans of different sizes and shapes, a metal basket, and a painted wooden cutout of a "sunbonnet girl" who holds a watering can. A colorful hooked rug brings all the colors together.

Make-It-Yourself

PAINTING & AGING METAL & TERRA COTTA

While you wouldn't want to change the appearance of a valuable collectible or treasured keepsake, the appearance of lots of run-of-the-mill, mass-produced items (both old and new) can be improved with paint. Adding color and an aged appearance to new metal and terra cotta containers is simple.

You'll Need:

A container – watering can, bucket, clay pot

Spray primer

Acrylic or latex paint in the color of your choice

Brown umber glaze or antiquing medium

Paint brush

Rags

Here's How:

1. Clean surface by wiping with a damp rag – it should be free of dust, dirt, and grease.

2. Apply a coat of primer to help the paint adhere better and prevent chipping. Allow to dry.

3. Paint the item with the acrylic or latex paint color of your choice. Allow to dry. Add a second coat, if needed, and allow to dry.

4. For an aged look, use a rag to apply brown glaze of antiquing medium, allowing the color to settle in the crevices of the piece. Or use a paint brush and this dry brush technique – dip the brush in glaze, blot on a rag to remove most of the glaze, and brush the glaze over the surface. ❑

"EARTH LAUGHS IN FLOWERS"

— GERTUDE JEKYLL

A painted wooden tray, *above*, is a moveable centerpiece planter when filled with an array of woodland mosses, flowering plants, and antique gardening tools. The center piece of the tray is an antique clothes iron.

Use the unexpected to surprise and delight. An old iron cradle from France holds a window box of blooms, *right*. Because the cradle sits high above the ground, it adds a whole new level to the garden. The front porch lattice is a perfect backdrop.

Aged Metal Makes Beautiful Planters

Metal containers don't weigh as much as their concrete counterparts, so they're more portable, and they won't freeze and crack in winter weather. Regular application of paints and sealers can keep rust at bay, but letting the metal age naturally outdoors has undeniable appeal.

The painted metal planter, *below*, adds a refined, classical touch that contrasts with its rustic setting. Its rust spots only add to the charm. An asparagus fern spills gracefully over the edge.

A cast iron birdbath, *right*, makes an elegant planter, indoors or out.

A tall, elegant garden urn is brought indoors and used as a vase for a bouquet of lilies.

Rather than discard a large damaged terra cotta pot, use it to spur your creativity. Here, a smaller pot is angled inside a larger pot and covers the break near the rim. A variety of shade-loving plants, trailing vines, and ferns are planted around a metal trellis for a stunning indoor display. Small concrete statues peek out from the lovely flowers.

The most common items can be transformed into unique planters. Two old cowboy boots – they're not even a pair – aren't for walkin' anymore, *above*. Slip water containers inside and add rooted cascading ivy vines for a fun, funky accent that's sure to be an eyecatcher.

Looks like this grocery buggy, *right*, never left the floral department! Spray painted white, cleverly lined with sheet moss, and filled with soil, this common item makes an interesting planter for growing all sorts of greenery in a movable display.

Sheds, Cottages & Barns

Formal and sophisticated or loose and casual, sheds, cottages, and barns can be inviting multi-purpose outbuildings that reflect you and your love of gardening and living things. Each structure is unique to the individual who creates it; whether you desire a formal cottage retreat or a well-utilized backyard hideaway, you can embellish it inside and out with things you love.

Buckets, barrels, and baskets are both decorative and functional – use them to store gloves, seed packets, and magazines for inspiration. Hang dried flowers tied with beautiful ribbons, or drape vintage fabrics, linens, and quilts on walls or over cabinet doors for a bit of romance.

An area initially intended for work can quickly become a favorite haven. I saw this immediately in the garden sheds I visited. Antiques and collectibles can make a potting shed a backyard getaway where one longs to visit and linger.

At right: This old wooden cart is a wonderful container for a mass of blooming flowers. Change the contents to greet the seasons with pumpkins in the fall, evergreens in the winter.

Nancy's Shed

This charming tin-roofed shed, *right,* is fun and inviting. Painted metal flowers and framed mirrors add interest and color to the wall around the painted blue door. Climbing vines soften the lines.

Along one side, *seen below,* a plank fence provides a perfect wall for hanging and displaying a collection of gardening paraphernalia, including tools and trellises, planters and hoses. An outdoor potting bench is close by and convenient.

A Marsh Cottage

This handsomely painted gardener's cottage is reminiscent of a picture postcard from New England. Window boxes spilling with vines and flowers and blooming shrubs in mulched beds add to the serenity. Choosing plants with blooms in one color family (here it's pink) is more restful to the eye than a riot of color.

Inside the cottage, dried flowers placed in a basket and hung on the whitewashed walls echo the soft colors of an old quilt. Garden tools are stored in a terra cotta pot.

Long-handled garden tools, *right,* make a functional, sculptural display when arranged against a fence or shed. Exposing tools to the elements will – over time – cause them to naturally rust and weather.

A table for two, *below,* with a tablecloth, patterned china, and fresh flowers, provides a restful retreat with a garden view.

A Meditation Cottage

A California cottage shed is striking inside and out. The porthole windows, gabled roof, and heraldic awning provide architectural interest. The whimsical spiral topiary and overflowing window boxes soften the angles.

Inside, gently faded floral fabrics are used to slipcover upholstered furniture and drape the windows. The white painted wooden plank walls are restful and provide a tranquil setting for reading or prayer.

Old Edna's Cottage Potting Shed

Like fine wine, the potting shed at the fanciful shop *Old Edna Says, "Well...La de Da"* has improved with age. Morning glories cascade from – and threaten to overwhelm – the roof. The shed and the garden around it are filled with treasures – collectibles, vintage china, painted furniture, and garden accessories – that are artfully displayed and available for purchase.

Inside Old Edna's Cottage Potting Shed

A folding rack originally intended for drying laundry, *below,* becomes a wonderful place to dry and display flowers and herbs. The garden theme is extended in the choice of the items displayed on top – an old enameled-tin coffee pot, a green-rimmed bowl, and a botanical print in a rustic frame. The white color further unifies the display.

At left, a cabinet with a distressed painted finish holds a variety of garden-themed collectibles.

Inside Old Edna's Cottage Potting Shed (cont.)

Gardening tools and supplies make a changeable display in the potting shed. Galvanized tin watering cans and troughs are both purposeful and pretty.

A low chest with peeling green paint makes an unusual, but perfectly useful, potting bench with lots of storage for supplies.

A planter with an interesting shape and peeling paint becomes a table with the addition of a glass top inside Old Edna's Cottage Potting Shed. Glass and mirror shops can cut glass to your specifications and polish the edges. Just think of the possibilities!

Metric Conversion Chart
INCHES TO MILLIMETERS AND CENTIMETERS

Inches	MM	CM		Yards	Meters
1/8	3	.3		1/8	.11
1/4	6	.6		1/4	.23
3/8	10	1.0		3/8	.34
1/2	13	1.3		1/2	.46
5/8	16	1.6		5/8	.57
3/4	19	1.9		3/4	.69
7/8	22	2.2		7/8	.80
1	25	2.5		1	.91
1-1/4	32	3.2		2	1.83
1-1/2	38	3.8		3	2.74
1-3/4	44	4.4		4	3.66
2	51	5.1		5	4.57
3	76	7.6		6	5.49
4	102	10.2		7	6.40
5	127	12.7		8	7.32
6	152	15.2		9	8.23
7	178	17.8		10	9.14
8	203	20.3			
9	229	22.9			
10	254	25.4			
11	279	27.9			
12	305	30.5			

Index